I Am Responsible

by Jenny Fretland VanVoorst

BLASTOFF! READERS

BELLWETHER MEDIA · MINNEAPOLIS, MN

Note to Librarians, Teachers, and Parents:

Blastoff! Readers are carefully developed by literacy experts and combine standards-based content with developmentally appropriate text.

Level 1 provides the most support through repetition of high-frequency words, light text, predictable sentence patterns, and strong visual support.

Level 2 offers early readers a bit more challenge through varied simple sentences, increased text load, and less repetition of high-frequency words.

Level 3 advances early-fluent readers toward fluency through increased text and concept load, less reliance on visuals, longer sentences, and more literary language.

Level 4 builds reading stamina by providing more text per page, increased use of punctuation, greater variation in sentence patterns, and increasingly challenging vocabulary.

Level 5 encourages children to move from "learning to read" to "reading to learn" by providing even more text, varied writing styles, and less familiar topics.

Whichever book is right for your reader, Blastoff! Readers are the perfect books to build confidence and encourage a love of reading that will last a lifetime!

This edition first published in 2019 by Bellwether Media, Inc.

No part of this publication may be reproduced in whole or in part without written permission of the publisher. For information regarding permission, write to Bellwether Media, Inc., Attention: Permissions Department, 6012 Blue Circle Drive, Minnetonka, MN 55343.

Library of Congress Cataloging-in-Publication Data

Names: Fretland VanVoorst, Jenny, 1972- author.
Title: I Am Responsible / by Jenny Fretland VanVoorst.
Description: Minneapolis, MN : Bellwether Media, Inc., 2019. | Includes bibliographical references and index.
Identifiers: LCCN 2018033447 (print) | LCCN 2018034233 (ebook) |
   ISBN 9781681036557 (ebook) | ISBN 9781626179301 (hardcover : alk. paper) |
   ISBN 9781618915016 (pbk. : alk. paper)
Subjects: LCSH: Responsibility–Juvenile literature.
Classification: LCC BJ1451 (ebook) | LCC BJ1451 .F74 2019 (print) | DDC 179/.9–dc23
LC record available at https://lccn.loc.gov/2018033447

Editor: Christina Leaf   Designer: Jeffrey Kollock

Printed in the United States of America, North Mankato, MN

Table of Contents

What Is Responsibility?

You said you would be home for dinner. But you want to play with your friend.

Do you skip dinner and play? Or are you responsible?

Responsible people do what is **expected** of them. They keep **promises**. They take care of their things.

Why Be Responsible?

It is not always easy to be responsible. Homework or **chores** may not be fun.

You do your work anyway. Other people **count** on you.

What if no one did what they needed to do? Nothing would get done!

Who Is Responsible?

You Are Responsible!

You can be responsible!
Put away your toys.
Brush your teeth.

Do what you need to do. Then you can do what you want to do.

You will feel
so grown up!

Glossary

chores

duties

expected

thought to be
reasonable or
necessary

count

depend

promises

statements made by
people that they will or
will not do something

To Learn More

AT THE LIBRARY

Cook, Julia. *But It's Not My Fault!* Boys Town, Neb.: Boys Town Press, 2015.

Murray, Julie. *Responsibility.* Minneapolis, Minn.: Abdo Kids, 2018.

Raatma, Lucia. *Responsibility.* Ann Arbor, Mich.: Cherry Lake Publishing, 2014.

ON THE WEB

Factsurfer.com gives you a safe, fun way to find more information.

1. Go to www.factsurfer.com.

2. Enter "responsible" into the search box.

3. Click the "Surf" button and select your book cover to see a list of related web sites.

Index

The images in this book are reproduced through the courtesy of: Pressmaster, front cover; John t, pp. 2-3, 22-24; Zurijeta, pp. 4-5, 6-7; Fertnig, pp. 8-9; PeopleImages, pp. 10-11; FatCamera, pp. 12-13; Dmitri Ma, pp. 14-15; L Julia, p. 15 (good, bad); DGLimages, pp. 16-17; kate_sept2004, pp. 18-19; Steve Debenport, pp. 20-21; granata68, p. 22 (top left); nd3000, p. 22 (middle left); Catchlight Visual Services/ Alamy, p. 22 (top right); Anurak Pongpatimet, p. 22 (bottom right).